3-

RAY

You might find this amusing.

Best Wishes for Christmas

'We are amused'

The Cartoonists' View
of Royalty

Edited and introduced by
PETER GROSVENOR

Foreword by H.R.H.
THE PRINCE OF WALES

THE BODLEY HEAD
LONDON   SYDNEY
TORONTO

British Library Cataloguing
in Publication Data
'We are amused'
1. English wit and humour, Pictorial
2. Windsor, House of – Caricatures and
cartoons
I. Grosvenor, Peter
741.5′942   NC1476
ISBN 0-370-30139-0

This selection © The Bodley Head Ltd 1978
Introduction © Peter Grosvenor 1978
Printed in Great Britain for
The Bodley Head Ltd
9 Bow Street, London WC2E 7AL
by William Clowes & Sons Ltd, Beccles
set in Monophoto Ehrhardt
First published 1978

ACKNOWLEDGMENTS

The Queen's Silver Jubilee Trust benefits from all the profits of this book and thanks are due to the many unpaid hands who made it possible—not least the cartoonists who gave freely of their works and the newspaper proprietors who have waived any reproduction charges.

The book grew out of an exhibition of Royal Cartoons, '*Not By Appointment*', which Prince Charles opened at the London Press Club in November 1977. Some months previously Christopher Joll of the Ideas Committee of the Queen's Silver Jubilee Appeal was lunching at the club looking for fund-raising ideas when his eye alighted on the club's splendid collection of cartoon originals which line the walls. 'Why not hold a Royal cartoon exhibition in aid of the Appeal?' he suggested. The idea was eagerly taken up by the then Club Secretary Terence Wright, and by the former Hon. Social Secretary Patricia Latham, who then chaired the organising committee.

From them came the idea of a book based on the exhibition. Keith Mackenzie, cartoon editor of Associated Newspapers, organised the selection and hanging of the cartoons at the exhibition and played a big part in assembling this book, as did John Jensen of The Sunday Telegraph and Alec Harrison, literary agent and Chairman of the Club at the time of the exhibition.

We should also like to record our gratitude to the Club President the Hon. Vere Harmsworth for his active support, to Hugh Richmond who enthusiastically represented the President on the organising committee and to Guy Pearse and Rob Stuart.

Not least do we thank HRH The Prince of Wales for his foreword to the book and for allowing us to use a selection of cartoons from the private album which was presented to him when he opened the exhibition.

P.G.

Acknowledgments are due to the following for permission to reprint copyright material:

Associated Newspapers Group Ltd, Coventry Evening Telegraph, The Daily and The Sunday Telegraph Ltd, Express Newspapers Ltd, Harpers and Queen, Mirror Group Newspapers, Morning Star, News International Ltd, The Observer, Private Eye, Syndication International, Times Newspapers Ltd, Titbits, United Newspapers Ltd, the National Portrait Gallery, the Press Club, Mrs Gerard Hoffnung and Dennis Dobson Ltd, John Murray (Publishers) Ltd.

The two Topolski drawings appeared originally in *The London Spectacle of 1935* by Feliks Topolski and D. B. Wyndham-Lewis, published by The Bodley Head.

BUCKINGHAM PALACE

Foreword by HRH
THE PRINCE OF WALES

I am only writing this foreword in order to show that I have a well-developed sense of humour and if proof is needed I can assure the readers of this book that I *opened* the exhibition of cartoons that inspired this publication. I have always felt that an ability to laugh at yourself is an essential requirement for a sane existence in this world. The same applies to our national life. Cartoonists, almost more than anyone else, help to relieve unnecessary tension, deflate ridiculous pomposity and emphasise the funny side of something that may threaten to become dangerously serious. It is also considerably easier to libel someone pictorially (and get away with it) than it is to do so by the printed word!

This book comprises an intriguing collection of 'royal' cartoons mostly from the past 25 years and shows the changes which have taken place in that period in both style and approach to the subject. Looking at them I cannot help but reflect on how politely we have been treated, compared to the way in which King George III and his family, for instance, were treated by the 18th and 19th century cartoonists, such as Rowlandson.

However, even if the cartoonists have shown, here and there, a dash of irreverence or a bite of satire, they obviously do not mean it *too* seriously because the Press Club have most generously offered the proceeds from this book to The Queen's Silver Jubilee Appeal. As Chairman of this Appeal I am extremely grateful for such a kind gesture and promise to retain my sense of humour for at least another 25 years. . . .

Charles.

THE CHANGING
FACE OF THE ROYAL CARTOON
by Peter Grosvenor

When you think of Gillray's attacks on Royalty, or even Sir Max Beerbohm's savage caricatures of a corpulent Edward VII, today's Royal Family, by comparison, is treated with a genteel touch. Well, largely . . .

Princess Anne's speeding offences, Prince Philip's occasional outspoken utterances on 'a bloody awful newspaper' or most recently the perils of Big Brother society, Prince Charles's girl friends—all have been the subject of a little mocking fun.

But today there is nothing to compare with Gillray's scathing caricature of the thirty-year-old Prince of Wales (later George IV) as the bloated voluptuary (page 56), in which disrespect and malice are present in every line. When George IV died *The Times* wrote: 'There can hardly be a wet eye in the kingdom for this debauched monarch.'

Perhaps the change in attitude is not too surprising. For Royalty itself has changed so much. It is less politically involved now and therefore a less controversial and legitimate butt of public criticism. It can scarcely be accused of extravagance when the Queen's Civil List at less than £3,000,000 a year mostly goes in staff wages and would in any case not pay for the droop-snoot of Concorde. Royalty has become, compared with a century ago, both more respected and loved. So, too, and this perhaps is surprising, have the cartoonists—or most of them. These days their work is praised as art and profound social commentary. Sometimes these supposedly satirical scourges of the establishment are even knighted.

It was not always so. Gillray was regarded as a scurrilous chap. When a life of him appeared in 1831 *The Athenaeum* commented scathingly of all caricaturists: 'Who would wish to know of the haunts and habits of a sort of private and public spy . . . who insults inferiority of mind and exposes defects of body?' Cartoonists of these times had, too, only a very limited circulation. The large crowds that gathered outside Mrs Humphrey's print shop in St James's Street to inspect the latest productions of Gillray or Cruikshank were small compared with the audience that later cartoonists commanded when *Punch* hit the bookstalls. And the *Punch* audience was small compared to what occurred at the very end of the last century when mechanical reproduction was advanced enough to allow cartoons in the newly emerging mass circulation papers. By then, whether the cartoonist liked it or not, there were the restraints imposed on his work by the editor, who in turn took his cue from his mass public. It is all right to irritate and provoke your readers, but not to lose them. In any case the mood of the times was increasingly jingoistic and patriotic.

None of this, however, applied to the earlier part of Queen Victoria's reign. Indeed she was subject to sharp criticism for being so reclusive after Albert's death. Leading public figures like Jo Chamberlain could talk seriously and openly of Republicanism.

As late as the Queen's Golden Jubilee, the famous caricaturist Phil May was doing crude political drawings of Queen Victoria for the *Sydney Bulletin* which show her for instance signing, with a sadistic grin, the Irish Coercion Bill. Later still Victoria and her son were drawn by Max Beerbohm as lugubrious comic figures. 'The rare, the rather awful visits of Albert Edward, Prince of Wales, to Windsor Castle' reads the caption of one cartoon as the Prince stands dunce-like in the corner, face to the wall (page 18).

Beerbohm apart, Edward VII got off remarkably lightly with the cartoonists considering his playboy life-style. Despite the baccarat and the divorce scandals, and the occasional picture of the King strolling at Cannes with an unidentified lady, the cartoonists did little to question the respectability and marital purity of the Royal Family.

There were ripples of anti-Monarchy feeling in the Great War because of the Royal Family's German blood. One Labour MP referred to George V as 'a German pork butcher'. In 1915 occurred a very rare instance of the Royal Family actually trying to censor the work of a cartoonist, the famous Australian Will Dyson, whose popular book *Kultur Cartoons* caricatured the Kaiser in a highly unflattering way. According to *The Star* King George V and Queen Mary were 'so angry that the censors have received orders to "put the soft pedal" on all war cartoons in the magazines and newspapers. Their majesties at first demanded an absolute prohibition on any pictures "caricaturing and insulting" the German Emperor and the Crown Prince.'

George V like the Kaiser was, after all, a grandson of Queen Victoria. The War Office then made a ruling that the cartoons could not be sent to soldiers in the field. The King's action was roundly attacked by *The Star* as 'entirely selfish and it is absolutely at odds with English public opinion'.

But as the war progressed such criticisms faded. Bit by bit George V, who never missed anything to do with public duty, assumed the mantle of 'Grandpapa England' as today's Queen called him—a remote much-loved figure, broadcasting in that strange, bronchial, deeply affecting voice to the nation. What mean scribe or artist would care to cast aspersions on him? The nearest was a little court-jesterly fun—the King and Queen Mary both being fond of slightly risqué jokes. When Sir Edwin Lutyens designed the royal doll's-house for the Empire exhibition he had MG and GM inscribed on the pillows in the monarch's bedroom. 'What,' asked Queen Mary, 'does that stand for?' Replied Sir Edwin, 'May George? George May.' Edward VIII, who frequently failed to turn up when duty called, inherited such immense goodwill from his father's reign and occupied the throne so briefly that no cartoonists made any mark against him. In fact as the distinguished artist Edmond Kapp recalls following many hours with the Prince of Wales informally sketching him for an eventual portrait (page 76), he had several eminently caricaturable mannerisms, notably fiddling with his bow tie.

Then, as Sir Osbert Lancaster puts it: 'Everyone loved Queen Elizabeth so much and felt so sorry for George VI having to take the throne against his wishes that any real criticism was unthinkable'—especially after the remarkable heroism and dedication they displayed in the war years. By long habit now the Press was hypnotised into seeing Royalty without a wart upon it. There was even a convention of not depicting the face of a royal person in a humorous drawing.

Illingworth of the *Daily Mail*, who at this time was at the height of his fame as a superb draftsman and a trenchant cartoonist, recalls that Royal cartoons were quite different from any other.

'You seemed to put your top hat on when you drew Royal cartoons. I did very few of them and wished I could have avoided it. It was like drawing a religious cartoon and I didn't do those very well either. It was not like today when people can be very rude. I am an old, old man, and in those days your editor and your readers expected solemn treatment of Royalty.'

The accession of a young Queen to the throne in 1952, in the circumstances of her father's early death at the age of only fifty-six, brought adulation of the Royal Family to a sentimental and near hysterical pitch. The then Minister of Works, Sir David Eccles, was roundly rebuked for referring to the Queen at Coronation time as 'a great leading lady', daring to imply that Royalty was a branch of show business rather than a direct link with the Almighty.

However, cartoonists, being by nature—and duty—irreverent, will not always be restrained. Few swam more strongly against the current than David Low in his Coronation cartoon in the *Manchester Guardian*. It appeared the day after the

Coronation and was entitled 'Morning After'. It pictured a battered and hung-over looking John Citizen after a one hundred million pound debauch blearily gazing at the grim face of regal reality peering out of a TV screen (page 87). The letters came flooding in—mostly very angry. 'Scandalous and vulgar', 'the humour of a very small minority who only harbour envy, hatred and malice in their hearts. What execrable bad taste!' coupled with the usual comments that, of course, 'The Queen cannot defend herself'.

Of course, the Queen can defend herself indirectly either through spokesmen or through members of her family who can speak most trenchantly when the occasion demands. But the public sensitivity to criticism of the Royal Family is still acute—not so much with the *Guardian* or *Observer* readers any more, but certainly among the more conservative readers of, say, the *Mail* or *Telegraph*.

Jensen of the *Sunday Telegraph* (one of the many Australians who have made their home here as cartoonists) recalls that readers took violent exception to what he intended to be a fairly flattering cartoon of the Queen. A ghostly Queen Elizabeth I addressed the much travelled Queen Elizabeth II in these words: 'My more spirited subjects used to globetrot while *I* stayed at home. What are all *your* Sir Walter Raleighs doing?' (page 73). What indeed—impeccable, true blue sentiments. A veritable Philippic, you might say. But readers were outraged that the Queen should have been caricatured at all as a middle-aged woman. 'Her Majesty was represented as an unattractive, frumpish woman, which she certainly is not,' grumbled one reader. And numerous others felt that any cartoon of royalty at all was tasteless and unnecessary. 'All I did,' protested Jensen, 'was to try to draw the Queen accurately, as a middle-aged woman.' He was mollified shortly afterwards, however, when a request came from Buckingham Palace, on behalf of Prince Philip, for the original of the drawing!

The Queen is in fact not the easiest person to caricature. Michael Cummings of the *Daily Express*, undeniably one of Her Majesty's most loyal subjects, says he always feels very inhibited.

'When you meet her she really is a very good-looking woman, fine eyes and complexion, charming smile. But photographs of her don't do her justice and caricatures, emphasising recognisable features of her like her teeth, can make her look ugly.'

Cummings reckons that the most difficult drawing of his life was the cartoon 'For Valour' which took up most of the front page of the *Express* after the Queen's visit to Ulster in August 1977 (page 32).

Queen Victoria presenting the Victoria Cross 'For Courage beyond the call of duty' was easy enough. 'But getting the expression right on the Queen's face was agony. The editor, then Roy Wright, didn't want her to look grim and yet a smile was inappropriate. After numerous tries I was still disappointed by the final result.'

Caricatures of Prince Charles almost invariably exaggerate his ears. This, too, caused Cummings uneasiness—especially when Charles was still at school. 'One reader wrote and said how beastly I was to make his ears so big, because now he'd be ragged unmercifully at school. I felt rather guilty.'

Cummings' attitude to Royalty is one he probably shares with millions of fellow citizens. 'When just about every other institution in this country is working badly, Royalty remains one of the things you can still truly admire.'

Less obviously reverential is Jon of the *Mail*, though he remembers in his early days with the old *Daily Graphic* that it was even *lèse-majesté* to draw a Royal face. 'I have few inhibitions now about caricaturing either Philip or the Queen— though I'm never vicious, hopefully just funny. I'll always feel free to have a go at Prince Philip because he does say some outrageous things. With the Queen that's different. You can't have her in politics.'

Mac of the *Mail* takes much the same line. 'One is not in business to offend the reader. But the strange thing is that when you think you might have offended they'll ask for a copy.'

New Zealander John Kent (yet another Antipodean cartoonist to have sought fame and fortune in Fleet Street) wears two hats—one on the *Mail* and another as the artist of the Varoomshka strip in the *Guardian* where he was one of the first to make jokes about Royal expenditure.

'I don't feel in the slightest degree inhibited about caricaturing Royalty.' Indeed in Varoomshka the Queen looks uncommonly like the Wicked Queen in Disney's 'Snow White'.

There are no complaints from *Guardian* readers. 'But I don't think the *Mail* readers would be too happy. David English the editor did once say to me that the Queen didn't look as nice as she might in one of my cartoons, so naturally one draws to suit one's market,' Kent added.

Mark Boxer—'Marc' of *The Times*—who has had several brushes with his editor William Rees-Mogg, is bound by similar considerations. 'I think jokes about Royalty are as valid as jokes about anyone else. But Mr Rees-Mogg does not agree, and there's very little point in my drawing a cartoon which I know stands no chance of being used. If the Royal Family don't answer back it's their choice not to do so, but I would always respect the Royal Family's private life.'

'Trog'—Wally Fawkes who draws the Flook strip in the *Mail*, and political cartoons on the *Observer*—reckons that 'no caricature should flatter, and I've never taken any special care not to make the Queen look ugly. One catches a humorous likeness and exaggerates exactly as one would do for anyone else. Royalty should be treated as people and not as related to God. It would be very insulting to make Charles's ears small. I used to get the odd complaint on the *Mail* but not on the *Observer*.'

New Zealander Keith Waite of the *Mirror* reckons that Trog was the pioneer of the modern-style Royal cartoon. 'He opened it up for all of us. I think there is room for Royal cartoons which are not as obsequious as the old top hat tradition but equally aren't as vicious as Gillray's. I try to strike that happy medium.'

Franklin of the *Sun*, who started his daily newspaper work with the old *Herald* and then with the *Mirror*, says it was Scarfe rather than Trog who made the major break-through. 'In my first few years on the *Mirror* you drew only the back view of the Queen. But after Scarfe's cartoons in *Private Eye* and to a lesser extent Steadman's—all the restrictions disappeared.

'It was the grotesqueness of Scarfe that was so startling. I remember one *Private Eye* cover of the Queen with enormous great teeth, sitting on a horse. It was cruel caricature, though his style, and from then on Fleet Street thought, if Scarfe can get away with this, we can at least start drawing Royalty from the front.

'Personally I favour the David Low style of drawing which goes more for likeness—I wouldn't draw the Queen's teeth as grotesque when they are plainly not. For me it's a question of keeping a close balance between realism and caricature.

'On the whole I think the Royal Family quite enjoy being pilloried. Prince Philip has asked for originals of several of my cartoons during Jubilee Year.'

Peter Maddocks, founder of the British Cartoonists Association, who has drawn for daily and Sunday newspapers, comments: 'The life of the cartoonist is easier now that the Queen is older. I mean now that she's wearing spectacles in public you no longer need to be so flattering.'

Barry Fantoni of *Punch* and *Private Eye* takes a more extreme view than that. 'I relish the opportunity to attack Royalty in every way. I'm a Republican. I'm not against the Queen personally, but I'm violently opposed to the institution. I can't attribute the graces of God to another human being.'

To be fair to the Royal Family it is a good few years (300 perhaps?) since they claimed any Divine Right. Prince Philip, blunt speaker as we know, told an audience in Ottawa on a Canadian tour: 'The answer to this question of monarchy is very simple—if the people don't want it they should change it. But let us end on amicable terms and not have a row. The monarchy exists not for its own benefit, but for that of the country. We don't come here for our health. We can think of better ways of enjoying ourselves.'

You can't say much fairer than that, and Prince Charles, talking to William Davis when the editor of *Punch*, made another crucial observation—about the ability to laugh at ourselves. 'If only more politicians were capable of laughing at themselves occasionally, the world would be a happier and more sensible place . . . As far as I am concerned a sense of humour is what keeps me sane and I would probably have been committed to an institution long ago were it not for the ability to see the funny side of life.'

Of course *Punch* itself, ever since it was founded in 1841, has been an interesting barometer of our mood towards Royalty. It began as an irreverent, even scurrilous sheet 'cheerfully unfair to the Royal Family in general and to Prince Albert in particular'.

Later it was to plumb the depths of obsequiousness—a servile Mr Punch telling George V on his accession: 'I know, Sir, that you will maintain the prestige of the Title. It would be impossible to increase it.'

Under Malcolm Muggeridge *Punch* began to shed its ageing conservative readership in favour of the younger, trendier readership profile so beloved of the advertisers and with that shift went a much more robust attitude to Royalty. Trog showing the Queen asleep at a Royal Performance, Princess Anne in the guise of a Centaur, etc.

'My own view is that Royalty should be caricatured exactly as anyone else,' says *Punch*'s Art Editor William Hewison. 'If it's good of its kind and fair comment we will do it. But I see no point in vicious satire. You might as well have a go at the RSPCA.'

Curiously enough an old Socialist, Giles of the *Daily Express*, probably best epitomises the national feeling on Royalty today.

'I make a distinction between pulling their legs and taking the mickey. The first is fun, the second is snide.

'I don't begrudge the Queen any of my taxes for Trooping the Colour. I'd rather see my money go on that than a Blue Streak rocket that won't go off—or even worse one that does go off. We would get greyer and greyer without the Royal Family. Thank God for 'em.'

'Try not to blame her, mother—perhaps it was too late to re-
route the walkabout . . .'

The rare, the rather awful visits of Albert Edward, Prince of Wales, to Windsor Castle.

If by some parental piece of folly,
Queen Victoria had been christened Dolly,
I wonder if the aura of her name
Would have been quite the same?

'Run like hell! Prince Philip
is out conserving wildlife.'

In the old days
if a Prince didn't find
the joke funny,
you lost your head..

calman

'I still can't understand how
he could have picked up yours
by mistake.'

'Well, it'll be the end
of an era for *me*!'

'If anything,
business is worse.'

'I was given to understand
it was just an honorary rank.'

'Excuse me! Are drag artistes permitted to curtsey?'

'On your toes everybody—here comes Mr Delfont!'

'On in five minutes, Marm!'

'Well, it has been an exhausting year!'

▶*A major theme of the 1974 elections was Who Rules Britain?*
—government or unions or . . .

'I still say that we're not a true democracy till we get a
Northerner in there.'

▶ *The Queen first wore spectacles in public at the State Opening of Parliament in Canada in 1977.*

►*The Queen visits Ulster.*

For Valour.

► *Almost the only discordant voices over the 1953 Coronation came from the Bevanites—left-wing Labour MPs who followed Aneurin Bevan.*

If the Bevanites ran the Coronation . . .

'Relax!—departure's delayed for an hour, the Duke has just found out they can get a cheap-day return after 9.30.'

'What are they like on Wagner's Ring?—there's a points failure at Haywards Heath.'

'Well, sir, since Manchester United were at home today that only leaves . . .'

► *Robert Dighton 1752–1814 was a prolific artist of the London scene and to his caricatures of London life he added military and political cartoons in the 1780s.*

Pub.ᵈ Octᵣ 25ᵗʰ 1810.

George the-IIIʳᵈ aged-72-1810.
REIGN'D-50-Years. A ROYAL JUBILEE.
Taken at Windsor by R Dighton. Spring Gardens.

'My husband and I . . .'

► *William Hamilton, Labour MP for Fife Central, is Parliament's most persistent critic of Royals and Royal expenditure.*

'Her Majesty has nothing against you personally, Mister Hamilton, but for your own protection thinks it best . . .'

► *Prince Charles had just started at Cheam, his first school.*

'Look what I got from a boy at school . . .!'

'Well, one thing's certain—they don't carry money.'

'I don't know quite how to tell you this, dearest Albert, but it
seems you're not going to make the Jubilee.'

"'Ello, Fingers, wot 'ave yer nicked today?'

In 1967 Barry Fantoni was asked to predict the Prince's life in pictures for Nova. He scored a bull's-eye in predicting the Navy and a beard, but Charles the racing driver, space man and monarch have yet to be.

► *A well-publicized photograph of Prince Charles in 1977 seemed to
indicate that he was thinning on top—heir not so apparent.*

'I don't care if he does need a toupée for Royal Ascot . . .!'

'There must have been one hotel he could have found a room in!'

'No baby of mine's going to be pushed around in a pram!'

'Knowing Gerry's reputation I wasn't taking any chances!'

'Hang on, Sir . . . my mistake . . . you're Admiral
of the Fleet today!'

"SOMETHING MUST BE DONE."
The Prince of Wales 1930's

"SOMETHING MUST BE DONE"
Prince Phillip 1970's

► *Giles's 'Grandma as Britannia' was the symbol for the cartoon exhibition at the National Portrait Gallery in 1970.*

Grandma as Britannia

'We popped our heads up to have our picture taken by Prince
Philip and got two barrels off Lord Snowdon.'

GILES, 1977

'Damn Joneses—he's wearing a *white* tie!'

54

► *While at Trinity College, Cambridge (where Lord 'Rab' Butler was Master) Prince Charles first learned to fly.*

'Ask His Royal Highness to come to my office when he's finished his solo flight.'

► *George IV was much derided as monarch. He was also a ready butt for cartoonists as Prince of Wales, when this scathing cartoon was drawn.*

A VOLUPTUARY *under the horrors of Digestion.*

'It's an invitation to a cocktail party . . .'
'I've got nothing to wear . . .'

► *This belligerent Welsh dragon symbolised a resurgent Welsh Nationalism.*

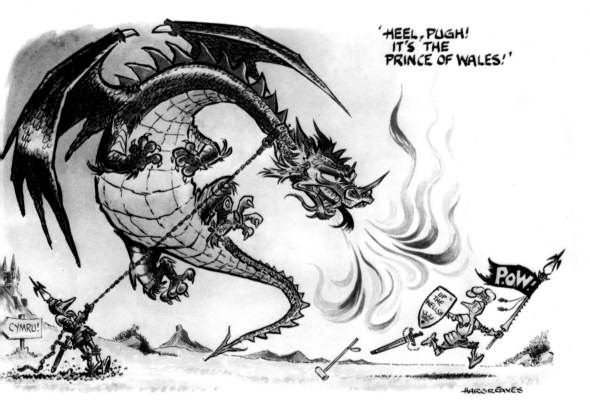

Royal Progress: a change in style

'And this is the Earls Court jester.'

JUBILEE

An American View
Copyright 1977 by Herblock in *The Washington Post*

'Frankly, I prefer the ones Prince Philip makes.'

'How many days sick leave do we have left this year?'

'Surprise!'

'Well, we ought to take them something.'

► *King George VI had just had a serious operation.*

'The Nation's Heart'

'She's demanding parity with the Midland car workers!'

'The Palace demands to know the source of this scurrilous
farrago of lies!'

'You must excuse my equerry—it's his first Royal Tour to
New Zealand!'

'Honestly, Norman, I much preferred your collection for my
American Tour.'

'My more spirited subjects used to globetrot while *I* stayed at
home. What are all *your* Sir Walter Raleighs doing?'

'Charles, I've told you before—"Sospan fach" is *not* the
National Anthem.'

► *Princess Caroline of Monaco's engagement had just been announced.*

► *Kapp, an observant artist, noticed that the Duke of Windsor, when Prince of Wales, had a nervous habit of toying with his bow tie.*

'You know, the size which fits into an Earl's coronet and still leaves room for a pack of biscuits and an apple.'

'How on earth *can* I pick up my skirt when that ghastly little Viscountess in the row behind kicked my shoes out of reach!'

'So would *you* flake out after a Royal walkabout . . .'

'If it's a boy, how about calling him Mark 2?'

'I'll be at my Mum's for the week-end—you
know her address . . .'

My Factory and I

► *The Duke of Windsor as 36-year-old Prince of Wales.*

The Prince of Wales at Biarritz

Morning After

'Cheer up, sunshine—sleeping through the lot isn't so bad.
There's always the Golden Jubilee in 2002.'

'"... and my total earnings for 1973–74 were ..." oh, dear, I
seem to have someone's tax forms mixed up with my speech.'

'Right. That's £150,000 on coal, £60,000 on candles and
£80,000 on fire extinguishers . . .'

► *How Macpherson of the Toronto Star saw the problem of 'Free Quebec' during the Royal visit in October 1977. While the Queen is preoccupied with Premier Trudeau the Quebec Premier René Lévesque makes a quick grab.*

► *There has been recurring speculation that Prince Charles might marry a commoner.*

'Sally Atkins of all people—How's your luck, luv?'

'I like the lad, Liz, but where will he get a mortgage on £2,000
a year?'

► *The Queen wore spectacles in public for the first time in Canada in 1977.*

'Gone to luncheon—back in half-an-hour.'

'Excuse me, but would you mind telling me who it is that
we're waiting for?'

'Have you got any power behind the throne?'

'I still don't see why we couldn't have had the day off like
everyone else!'

'. . . and treble time for informal garden party handshakes
makes it exactly 980,000 . . .'

Lord Snowdon

'Put that gear back in the attic and stop showing off to the visitors.'

Survival of the Fittest

'Well . . . that was a great Coronation rehearsal!'

'You'd think the Queen 'ud give an amnesty to anyone getting
married today.'

'. . . and remember, he's the one chap we
don't have to sell Concorde to.'

'Don't worry, sir, lots of us 'ave to start off livin' with the
in-laws.'

► *Trog designed this 'coat of arms' for the cartoon exhibition*
'Not by Appointment'.

'Is it really true that one day all this will be mine?'

'Who won the two-thirty at Epsom?'

► *Harold Macmillan, in his first year as Premier, and Selwyn Lloyd.*

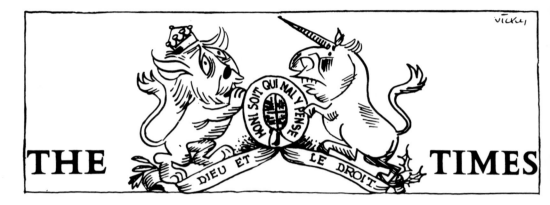

'You are supposed to hold your street party in *your* street,
not hers.'

'It's just a question of getting them involved in more exciting things,' says Prince Charles discussing football hooligans.

'Whatever makes you think it's Princess Anne's?'

► *The BBC's 50th birthday coincided with the Queen's 25th wedding anniversary.*

'I sometimes think the BBC are overdoing *their* anniversary.'

The Lifer

Elegantia cum Utilitate

INDEX OF ARTISTS